Sloth Bears

ABDO
Publishing Company

Big
Buddy BOOKS
Asian Animals

by Julie Murray

VISIT US AT
www.abdopublishing.com

Published by ABDO Publishing Company, PO Box 398166, Minneapolis, Minnesota 55439.

Copyright © 2013 by Abdo Consulting Group, Inc. International copyrights reserved in all countries. No part of this book may be reproduced in any form without written permission from the publisher. Big Buddy Books™ is a trademark and logo of ABDO Publishing Company.

Printed in the United States of America, North Mankato, Minnesota.
092012
012013

 PRINTED ON RECYCLED PAPER

Coordinating Series Editor: Rochelle Baltzer
Editor: Marcia Zappa
Contributing Editors: Megan M. Gunderson, Grace Hansen, Sarah Tieck
Graphic Design: Maria Hosley
Cover Photograph: *Getty Images*: David Courtenay.
Interior Photographs/Illustrations: *Animals Animals-Earth Scenes*: Ghani, Khalid (p. 21), Leszcznski, Zigmund (p. 13); *Fotosearch.com*: © Yippikaye (p. 11); *Getty Images*: Elliot Neep (p. 17), Gavin Parsons (pp. 5, 7, 29); *iStockphoto*: ©iStockphoto.com/gnagel (p. 11), ©iStockphoto.com/JohnnyGreig (p. 8), ©iStockphoto.com/HU-JUN (p. 4), ©iStockphoto.com/Sisoje (p. 9), ©iStockphoto.com/Wtolendars (p. 9); *Minden Pictures*: E.A. Kuttapan/npl/Minden Pictures (p. 27); *naturepl.com*: ©Nick Garbutt (p. 19), ©Axel Gomille (p. 25); *Photo Researchers, Inc.*: David Husking (pp. 15, 23); *Shutterstock*: Stephane Bidouze (p. 21), Image Focus (p. 4), Rudolf Tepfenhart (p. 9), Brian Upton (p. 23).

Library of Congress Cataloging-in-Publication Data

Murray, Julie, 1969-
  Sloth bears / Julie Murray.
      p. cm. -- (Asian animals)
  ISBN 978-1-61783-557-5
  1. Sloth bear--Juvenile literature. I. Title.
  QL737.C27M897 2013
  599.78--dc23
                          2012023975

Contents

Long ago, nearly all land on Earth was one big mass. About 200 million years ago, the land began to break into **continents**. One of these continents is Asia.

Sloth bears are known for their messy looks and loud eating habits.

Asia is the largest **continent**. It includes many countries and **cultures**. It also has different types of land and interesting animals. One of these animals is the sloth bear. In the wild, these bears are only found in Asia.

Sloth Bear Territory

Sloth bears are found in South Asia. They live in low hills and valleys in many different **habitats**. These include rocky areas, grasslands, and dry or wet forests.

Bhutan

Nepal

India

Sri Lanka

Sloth Bear Territory

Uncovered!
There are two types of sloth bears.
These are the Indian and the Sri Lankan
sloth bear. They are very similar.

Sloth bears look for habitats with
large rocks and trees for shelter.

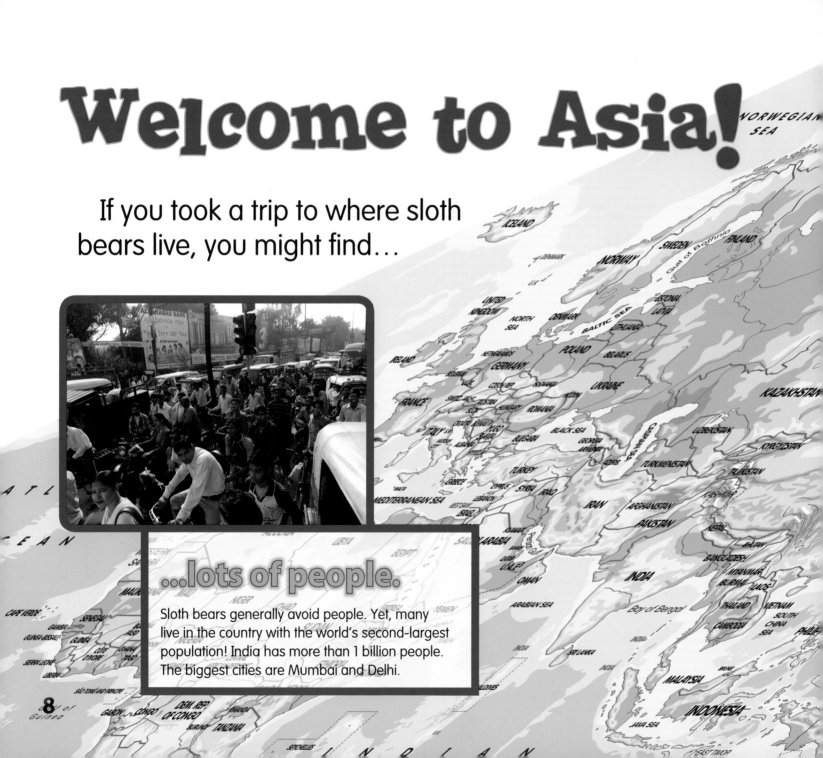

Welcome to Asia!

If you took a trip to where sloth bears live, you might find…

…lots of people.

Sloth bears generally avoid people. Yet, many live in the country with the world's second-largest population! India has more than 1 billion people. The biggest cities are Mumbai and Delhi.

...religion and art.

The three main religions in South Asia are Buddhism, Islam, and Hinduism. These have led to the creation of many beautiful works of art. These include statues, temples, and buildings such as India's Taj Mahal (*right*).

...many languages.

Many different languages are spoken in South Asia. One common language is Hindi. It uses a different alphabet from English. The Hindi alphabet has 44 letters.

प्रवेश
ENTRY →

...farms.

About two-thirds of the people in South Asia make a living as farmers. Sometimes, crops are grown on mountains on large steps called terraces (*left*). Important crops include rice, bananas, and coconuts. Sloth bears have been known to steal these crops.

Take a Closer Look

Sloth bears have rounded bodies. They have short, strong legs and long, curved claws. A sloth bear has two eyes, two round ears, and an extra-long snout.

Sloth bears are large animals. Adults are five to six feet (1.5 to 1.8 m) long. They stand two to three feet (0.6 to 0.9 m) tall at their shoulders. And, they weigh 120 to 310 pounds (55 to 140 kg). Males are larger than females.

A sloth bear's claws are about three inches (8 cm) long. They help the bear climb trees and get food.

Sloth bears have thick, **shaggy** fur. It is extra long around their necks and shoulders. These bears have dark fur. But, they have a light-colored U, V, or Y shape on their chests. And, they have light-colored **snouts** with almost no fur.

Most sloth bears have black fur. But, some have dark brown or dark red fur.

Female sloth bears share their home areas with their young.

Independent Life

Adult sloth bears generally live alone. Each one has a home area that is about eight square miles (21 sq km).

Sometimes, sloth bears share parts of their home areas. And, they visit one another's home areas to **mate**.

Sloth bears make meaningful faces and noises.
Their noises include roars, howls, yelps, and huffs.

Most sloth bears are active at night.
They sleep during the day. They do not
have one single home that they live in.
They use caves, dens, hollow trees, and
thick bushes for **shelter**.

Many bears hibernate, or sleep, through the winter. Sloth bears don't. This is because they can find food all year long.

Mealtime

Sloth bears eat many different foods.
They eat honey, flowers, and fruits such
as figs and mangoes. They also eat eggs,
small animals, and dead animals.

Most of all, these bears love to eat bugs!
They really enjoy ants and termites.

Sloth bears often have to climb trees to get fruit or honey.

19

Bug Eaters

Sloth bears are well built for eating bugs such as ants and termites. They use their strong legs and long, sharp claws to climb trees and hills. Then, they use them to tear open bug mounds or nests.

Termite mounds have rock-hard outer walls. They are made of mud and termite spit.

Sloth bears are the only bears that live almost entirely on bugs.

Sloth bears have **snouts** that move easily. They can wrap their lips tightly around holes in mounds or nests. Sloth bears don't have front teeth. So, they suck bugs up through the gap! And they have long, sticky tongues that are perfect for grabbing bugs.

Uncovered!
Sloth bears are very noisy eaters. Their sucking sounds can be heard hundreds of feet away!

Sloth bears can close their noses. This keeps out dirt and bugs while they eat.

Baby Bears

Sloth bears are **mammals**. Females usually have one or two babies at a time. They give birth in hollow trees or underground dens.

Baby sloth bears are called cubs. At birth, they weigh about 14 ounces (400 g). At first, cubs stay in their den. There, they drink their mother's milk and grow.

Cubs face many dangers. Tigers, wolves, and leopards hunt them. And, humans capture cubs to train as dancing bears for circuses and other shows.

After two to three months, sloth bear cubs are ready to leave the den. They ride on their mother's back while she finds food and eats. Cubs stay with their mother for two to three years.

Uncovered!
Sloth bear cubs even ride on their mother's back while she climbs trees!

Sloth bears are the only kind of bears that carry their young on their backs.

Survivors

Life in Asia isn't easy for sloth bears. New buildings and farms take over their **habitats**. Farmers kill the bears so they don't eat their crops. People also kill them to use their body parts in **medicine**.

Still, sloth bears **survive**. There are laws against killing them. And it is illegal to sell them to most countries. Sloth bears help make Asia an amazing place!

Uncovered!
Sloth bears are vulnerable. That means they are in some danger of dying out.

Sloth bears live up to 40 years in zoos.
They live about 20 years in the wild.

Wow!
I'll bet you never knew...

...that sloth bears are also called honey bears. They are well known for their love of this sweet treat. To get honey, a sloth bear will climb a tree and knock down a beehive. Then, it eats the honey out of it on the ground.

...that the character Baloo, from *The Jungle Book*, is likely based on the sloth bear. And his name comes from the Hindi word *bhalu*, which means "bear."

...that sloth bears were originally called bear sloths. The first European scientists to see them noticed their **shaggy** fur, long claws, and unusual teeth. They thought the animals were a type of sloth. Later, scientists realized that they were bears and changed their name.

Important Words

continent one of Earth's seven main land areas.

culture (KUHL-chuhr) the arts, beliefs, and ways of life of a group of people.

habitat a place where a living thing is naturally found.

mammal a member of a group of living beings. Mammals make milk to feed their babies and usually have hair or fur on their skin.

mate to join as a couple in order to reproduce, or have babies.

medicine (MEH-duh-suhn) an item used in or on the body to treat an illness, ease pain, or heal a wound.

shaggy made up of long, tangled hair or fur.

shelter to be covered or guarded.

snout a part of the face, including the nose and the mouth, that sticks out. Some animals, such as sloth bears, have a snout.

survive to continue to live or exist.

Web Sites

To learn more about sloth bears, visit ABDO Publishing Company online. Web sites about sloth bears are featured on our Book Links page. These links are routinely monitored and updated to provide the most current information available.

www.abdopublishing.com

Index